ISBN: 978-1-7638379-4-2 (Paperback)
ISBN: 978-1-7638379-3-5 (eBook)

Published by Jim Nicholls
Copyright © Jim Nicholls 2025

DEDICATED UNTO DEATH

The Matthew Connolly Story

By
JIM NICHOLLS

Table of Contents

Introduction

The year is 1817

IN AUSTRALIA, Federation is still a long way off; Queensland is regarded as part of the colony of New South Wales, and will remain so until 1859 even though public meetings are already being held to consider Queensland's separation from New South Wales.

On 6 June 1859, Queen Victoria signed Letters Patent to form the colony of Queensland. A proclamation to that effect was read by Sir George Bowen on 10 December of that year whereupon Queensland was formally separated from New South Wales.

On the other side of the world, in Galway, County Galway, Ireland a baby boy, later to be named Matthew Connolly was born. In 1845, then aged twenty-eight, he married Catherine Carroll. Matthew was a hard worker and a good provider for his growing family which soon numbered four with the addition of daughter Henrietta and son Matthew. But he had bigger plans which included moving away from Ireland, settling in Australia and starting a new life in the new colony of Queensland.

European settlement had begun in 1824 when a convict outpost was established at Redcliffe. The settlement was transferred to the northern bank of the Brisbane River the following year and continued to operate as a penal establishment until 1842 when the remaining convicts were withdrawn and the district opened to free settlement. By then squatters had already established themselves on the Darling Downs, far from the seat of government in Sydney. Agitation soon began over the creation of a separate northern colony which could manage its own local interests. The clamour for such a move was loudest in the fledgling township of Brisbane.

Most vocal among those seeking representative government was the Reverend John Dunmore Lang, member for Moreton Bay in the New South Wales Legislative Council. However, Lang's call for the creation of a northern colony was defeated in the Council in 1844 by twenty-six votes to seven. Matters were held in abeyance until 1850 when the British Parliament passed the Australian Colonies Government Act, enabling the creation of new Australian colonies with similar forms of government to New South Wales. This meant they would have a bicameral parliament overseen by a vice-regal representative. Importantly, specific mention was made of Port

Phillip and Moreton Bay as districts likely to become colonies in the foreseeable future.

The passing of the Act inspired Lang to renew his efforts. Between 1851 and 1854 he held nine meetings to gain further support for separation. He was, in fact, preaching to the converted as the inhabitants of the northern district had been increasingly neglected by the government in Sydney. However, while they could reach consensus on the need for separation, debate centred on whether a new colony would be 'free' or 'unfree' became a divisive issue. Lang and the majority of townspeople favoured free immigration. While urban growth in Brisbane and Ipswich finally decided the former, the powerful squatting fraternity, heavily reliant on cheap labour, advocated a renewal of convict transportation. Also, disagreement remained over where the new capital should be situated.

Brisbane, Toowoomba, Rockhampton, Cleveland, Gayndah, Gladstone and Ipswich were all potential candidates, favoured of course by parochial interests. Brisbane eventually emerged victorious, and the reality of a new colony moved a step closer. In 1856 the British Government agreed the time was ripe to create a new northern colony. Then, among other things there was uncertainty and debate as to the location of a southern border; it was eventually fixed at its present location.

Lang was among many others who believed the Northern Rivers region should become part of a northern colony. Although the New South Wales Government disagreed, Queen Victoria finally stepped in and signed the Letters Patent, on 6 June 1859; Queensland came into being.

The following month, unofficial news was received that the Secretary of State for the Colonies, Sir Edward Bulwer-Lytton, had appointed Sir George Bowen to be the colony's first Governor. While both the Letters Patent and the Order-in-Council appointing Bowen as Governor were duly published by the New South Wales Government, separation could not be accomplished until the Letters Patent had also been published in Queensland. Even though Governor Bowen was not due to arrive until 6 December 1859 with the Letters Patent formally proclaiming the new colony, a reception committee was already being organised as early as September to arrange the grand celebrations.

Sir George Ferguson Bowen along with Lady Diamantina Bowen were duly

Chapter One:
To Australia

A COMMUNIQUE received from Liverpool, dated 22 February 1853 advised authorities in Australia that the next immigrant ship, *John Fielden* of nine hundred and sixteen tons was on the berth in that city, taking on passengers for Moreton Bay. It also advised that no cargo would be received.

The ship made an excellent run of ninety days from Liverpool from where she'd sailed on 11 March 1853. She reached the Cape of Good Hope in fifty-nine days, was off Sydney on the eighty-fourth day, and took the pilot on board inside Moreton Bay seven days later. She berthed on 19 June 1853.

The ship's log indicated that contact was made with the outward bound *Marco Polo* which had left Liverpool a day after the *John Fielden*. It was also recorded that during the voyage one of the vessel's supernumerary seamen jumped overboard for no apparent reason and drowned.

On coming into Moreton Bay, the skipper Captain Clarke was dismayed to find there were no buoys to mark the shipping channel, as shown upon his chart.

It appears that the buoys recently laid down were all carried away. He had no alternative but to idle around in the area where he thought the channel ought to be; waiting there until the pilot arrived and came on board. But, by then it was too hazy to proceed, and the captain was therefore obliged to anchor in the open sea channel. A consequence of that was the parting of the cable, forcing him to take another anchor. Next morning, adding to his woes, the windlass broke while the second anchor was being hoisted. Despite these mishaps the ship was finally brought over to the usual anchorage ground in the Brisbane River.

The original number of immigrants who had embarked was three hundred and ninety-three; there were four deaths and seven births on the passage. While on board the vessel, they were divided as follows: married couples, 73; single women 102; single men 19: males from 1 to 14 years, 42; females from 1 to 14 years, 76; and infants 14.

When the Health Officer had made his inspection and completed a satisfactory report, members of the local Immigration Board proceeded to the ship to muster the passengers, after which they were removed to Brisbane without delay. It will be seen that of the total number of passengers, only ninety-two are adult males, and of these seventy-three are married, the remainder being connected with families on board. The large number of single women and girls made it highly desirable for everyone requiring female servants to apply for them forthwith. This was to prevent excuses for terminating the immigration supply.

While on this subject, we cannot avoid alluding to reports which had long been current, to the effect that some parties employed in the Immigrant Depot at Brisbane were in the habit of taking great pains instructing newly arrived women servants to hold out for higher rates of wages, with the apparent object of benefitting the establishment and its members. There was real concern over such a practice. The *Moreton Bay Courier* in its issue of Saturday 18 June 1853 was most indignant: *We trust that these reports are unfounded, or, if true, that such an objectionable practice will be forthwith abandoned.*

The immigrants were recorded as being all well. At the time, the migrant contract price was twenty-one pounds, nineteen shillings.

The passenger list included:

51. Connolly Matthew (35) Farm Labourer, Galway;

52. Connolly Catherine (26) Wife;

53. Connolly Harriet (6);
54. Connolly Matthew (4).

The vessel was named in honour of **John Fielden** (1784–1849), a British industrialist and Member of Parliament. He was a proponent of shortening the working day, and sponsored the successful Ten Hours Act of 1847.

The *John Fielden*

Chapter Two:
Living the Dream

UPON ARRIVAL in Australia Connolly joined the New South Wales Mounted Police and became a constable in B Division of the Metropolitan Police Force. He was initially appointed to Ipswich where he remained for several years before being transferred to Gatton forty kilometres to the west. There, he was appointed by the Police Magistrate, Lieutenant-Colonel Charles George Gray to be the station's watch house keeper. At that time, the Queensland Governor had designated Gatton Police Station as a general receiving jail for all prisoners committed to either Ipswich or Brisbane. Those coming from country regions further west had to be processed through Gatton.

Connolly's appointment as watch house keeper at Gatton included, as part of his duties, escorting prisoners to Ipswich as required.

The family settled easily into their new environment; life was good. During their time in Queensland, Matthew and Catherine had another four children: William, John, Anna, and Paul.

Matthew Connolly received an allowance of eighteen to twenty pounds to purchase rations, wood, water, candles and other necessities.

In a letter to his sister back home, he told of the pleasant lifestyle he and the family were enjoying.

Gatton Police Station
15 October 1860

My ever dear Margaret,

I confidently hope you will pardon my apparent neglect in not having written before now. I would have done so but I have been a good deal tossed, and so has the entire Police force both Brisbane and Ipswich, particularly the older members of the establishment. It has originated from the fact of having a Governor, and this part being proclaimed Queensland. I lost my best and dearest old friend Colonel Gray, he has retired from the Police and resigned his Commission as Police Magistrate. However, previous to his retirement he appointed me watch house keeper at Gatton. It is a much better and easier situation than that of being in the Mounted Police, particularly as the Governor proclaimed Gatton as a general receiving gaol, and all prisoners committed either to Brisbane or Ipswich, must come here and quarter with the other. I have £18 to £20 to receive for rations, wood, water, and candles, etc.

It is a most healthy spot, free from mosquitoes and abounds with splendid freshwater fish and all sorts of game, lots of wild turkeys; it is the most fertile soil in all Queensland. I have beautiful gardens that I purchased from the constables I succeeded. Not one member that was in the force that you knew that but has either resigned or has been dismissed. But Harris is Sergeant of the Town or City of Ipswich. John Broderick is in my place; I resigned in his favour, for if he remained in Brisbane he would have been dismissed by the new inspector who came from Sydney. There are twenty constables in the City of Ipswich, there are Aldermen and a Mayor now there, and Broderick is not yet married. He was here the night that your letter came to hand. I read it for him, he filled with tears when he heard that your baby died, he is as good-natured as ever.

Catherine and all the youngsters send their love to you, particularly Henrietta, Mat, William and John. They are all greatly grown, particularly since they came to this fine healthy situation. We have got Anna Marcella since you left; she is two years and five months old. I called her after poor dear Mother, she is the flower of the flock, and the smartest and best looking. I am only here six months. Kate and Mat left here in June, she left to be confined, and has to remain in town for three months. She presented me with another fine boy who is three months old now. I called him after my uncle Paul.

Praise be to God, I was not so privileged as I am now, and am likely to be. I have as much potatoes and vegetables as I can use of all sorts, lots of melons, pumpkins and cucumbers. From the time I *plant my potatoes, in ten weeks they are fit to dig and have two crops in the year; I have become a very good gardener. There has been a land sale here the other day. I purchased two allotments in Ipswich and one here, and acre allotments here are selling for £8.*

This new colony called after our Queen, namely Queensland, will become the best part of the colony for a poor man to get on. The Governor is an Irishman and is very good to his country people. Lots of good employment, the roads are very good now and anyone that would be able to muster a horse team would make an excellent living by it. The Government has employed a party to explore this locality for gold. Should you and your man consider to come to this part, in the course of time he will do well. Shearers are getting 4s. 6d. per score this season; good and plenty if your man is what grated handy general bush man he would do well here. I will let you know all particulars in my next.

I never was so much surprised as I was a few days ago when I went to Ipswich to see Kate. She told me that Caulfield Waring called on her yesterday, and that she entertained him having spent all his money. It appears that his Aunt died and left him a legacy and he paid his wage with part and spent the remainder when he came to Ipswich. It was by chance that he made out Kate, otherwise the fool would be badly off. I brought him up here with me and kept him till I got him in a good situation as overseer of a road party at Rio near Ayr and rations. I went with him to meet my old friend Councillor Balcony, from Galway, who is one of the Members of Parliament for Brisbane. He has Anna Maria, Lizzie Ann Profeels with him. All the children he has is Lizzy Caulfield.

Poor Mother is still living in Portumna, and has young Caulfield with her. William is doing well, and is in the railway Police. I never heard from Anthony, God bless and let me know of his fate and say he is living. Answer this at once and I will then tell you all the news in reply at once.

I am joined by Kate and little ones in best regards for you and Andrew.

Your affectionate brother, Matthew Connolly.

Chapter Three:
The Good Colonel

IN THE letter to his sister, Connolly wrote of his best and dearest old friend, Colonel Gray.

Australia's past history is filled with many extraordinary characters. Gray is no exception.

Lieutenant-Colonel Charles George Gray was born in Edinburgh, Scotland on 28 November 1786. He obtained a commission as ensign in the 77th Regiment in 1796. Then, in 1800 a lieutenancy was purchased for him in the 78th Highlanders. In 1810 Captain Gray sailed with his regiment for Spain, where he fought in the Peninsular War, being twice wounded in the process.

As a young Scots officer in the British Army, he saw action in India, Spain, and Portugal, and was also present at the Battle of Waterloo in 1815.

In order to complete his education, he went on half pay to enable him to complete his education. In 1803 he was attached to the 75th Regiment on full pay. His appointment to this regiment owed much to the high esteem in which its officers held the memory of Lieutenant Gray's father, who commanded it in Guzerat, and who, while in command died there from fever brought on by exposure. A memorandum was sent by the officers of the 75th to his Royal Highness the Duke of York requesting his appointment to his father's old regiment. This was accordingly approved and gazetted; in 1804 he joined the regiment in Calcutta. He was present at the famous seventeen-day siege of Bhurtpore, where the 75th lost two thirds of its officers and men.

In 1809 Gray was appointed to a company in the third battalion of the 95th Regiment (Rifle Brigade) which joined the Peninsular Army in 1810. The regiment's three battalions took part in numerous major battles and skirmishes before returning home. Back in England he resumed his studies, and spent time as a student in the Military College at High Wycombe.

The Colonel was awarded the Peninsular Medal, with multiple clasps denoting campaigns in which he had seen action. He was, however, so heartily tired of the constant separation from his family, and with his health having suffered from a previous sojourn in India, he was allowed to sell out. He left the army in 1837 and moved with his family to settle in New South Wales.

After five arduous months on board the convict ship *John Barry*, the family finally reached Port Jackson. Their voyage to Australia was in stark contrast to the comparative comfort experienced by Matthew Connolly and his family sixteen years later.

The Gray family took up a land grant on the Hastings River near Port Macquarie north of Sydney where they remained until 1847. He served in a series of different appointments including, in 1851, that of Gold Receiver in the Sydney Treasury: a position he held until 1853. Moving on, he was appointed to the Police Magistracy of Ipswich, where he settled with his family. At that time there was no town council and the sole authority seems to have been the Police Magistrate. As well as presiding in court, he dispersed government money, reported on floods, supervised road repairs, and generally ran the place. He remained at that appointment until his retirement in 1866: completing service of both military and civil work of sixty years.

It was at Gray's home in East Street, Ipswich that Lady Bowen, wife of the Governor of Queensland, spent her first night in the town. Sir George and Lady Diamantina were undertaking their initial visit to Ipswich on 10 December 1859.

As a gallant soldier and as well as being one of the oldest veterans of the British Army, the Colonel commanded respect and veneration, not only as a brave warrior, but for the kindness and consideration he had shown towards those less fortunate members of society.

Lieutenant-Colonel Gray died on 7 September 1873, aged eighty-eight years. Having been the first captain gazetted to the Ipswich Company of the Queensland Volunteer Rifle Brigade, he was accorded a military funeral with full honours.

Matthew Connolly was not the only one who had been singing the colonel's praises. He was so popular with the people of Ipswich that his funeral was reported in the *Queensland Times* newspaper as being 'the most numerously attended one which ever occurred in Ipswich'. *The Ipswich Observer* (10 September 1873), wrote a long and glowing obituary, which showed the respect in which he was held.

On 23 July 2017 *Queensland Times* columnist Beryl Johnston penned an enthusiastic article entitled: *From the Battle of Waterloo to police magistrate of Ipswich; Military man who made a big impact.*

In his book *That Gallant Gentleman: the remarkable story of Colonel Charles George Gray,* Kenneth Dutton describes Gray as having

proved himself to be not only the Christian
hero but the Christian gentleman.

Chapter Four:
Tragedy

PRIOR TO Connolly's departure on a prisoner escort detail on Sunday 25 August 1861, Doctor Rowlands of Gatton asked him, while he was in Ipswich, to collect medication for two of his patients. The patients were Lady Joshua Bell who had become seriously ill while visiting friends at Grantham near Gatton; the other was Mrs Curry, wife of the police station's sergeant in charge.

By then, the constable had completed many such escort procedures and considered himself to be a bit of an 'old hand' at such a task. He arrived in Ipswich without incident and handed his prisoner over to the local police.

After three days in the larger establishment, he was ready to make the return journey to Gatton.

By the time Constable Connolly left Ipswich on 29 August, the local creeks and streams were swollen from the downpours which had inundated the region.

Connolly's intention was to leave Ipswich early that day and return to Gatton as quickly as possible to deliver the urgently needed medical supplies. The Old

Toowoomba Road, used by Connolly on the outward leg of his journey, was an established route between Laidley and Gatton. There were no other established or documented routes between these two towns in 1861, nor was there a route through Forest Hill, a small establishment located between the larger settlements. The railway line was not completed until 1866.

Returning along the way he had travelled a few days earlier, the constable reached Sandy Creek, about nine kilometres north-west of Laidley. It was around five o'clock in the afternoon. The creek was in full flood. An itinerant man, one of several camped on the Laidley side creek bank, tried to persuade him against even thinking of entering the swiftly flowing water.

'It's too high,' the man said. 'You'll never make it.'

Connolly took a few minutes to weigh up the situation.

'I've got urgent business to take care of,' he replied. 'I have to get across. It'll be okay.'

With the crossing point at Sandy Creek in flood, Connolly had no option but to put his horse to the raging torrent. A bypass at the time was not an option as Sandy Creek flowed north to low lying plains which were also flooded. Plus, there were no established alternate routes south of the crossing which, to find one, would mean travelling over steep, unmarked terrain. Therefore, it has been determined that the site at the intersection of Sandy Creek and Glen Cairn Road (Old Toowoomba Road), Glen Cairn is where Constable Connolly attempted to cross the creek in 1861.

His devotion to duty and the urgency associated with the medicine finally decided for him. He would press on.

Connolly tied two packages across his chest, and urging his horse forward, entered the water. However, within seconds he and his horse were swept off the crossing. He lost the grip on his mount; they were separated and the constable was dislodged from the saddle. The horse made for the opposite bank. Connolly was swiftly carried downstream. Bystanders tried to rescue him but he soon disappeared from view.

His body was located the following morning, some three hundred metres downstream from where he had entered the water the previous afternoon. In his pockets were the two small bottles of medicine.

*Looking towards the east, the creek crossing
north-west of Laidley where Connolly lost his life*

Lady Bell

One of the small glass containers of medicine which cost Connolly his life in 1861 was intended for a very important person. Lady Bell was the wife of Sir Joshua Peter Bell, speaker of the Legislative Assembly.

She was born in Clare, Ireland in 1841. In the days when Queensland was sparsely populated, and when its future was not too certain, she and her husband took over Jimbour Station near the present day town of Dalby. They were responsible for managing the property and constructing the glorious mansion which remains to this day as a major attraction. The small township of Bell, north of Dalby, is named in the family's honour.

The medicine which cost Constable Connolly his life must have worked. Lady Bell lived until 1915, dying suddenly of peritonitis. A glowing obituary in the *Dalby Herald* described her as an acknowledged beauty and a pioneer whose geniality and hospitality endeared her to all who met her. She was one of the pioneer women of Queensland, and one of the kindest and most endearing of them all.

Chapter Five:
Enquiry

A MAGISTERIAL enquiry into the cause of death of the late Gatton Constable Matthew Connelly was conducted at Laidley on 31 August 1861 (two days after the tragic event). The person in charge of proceedings was Mr William Rawson, one of Her Majesty's Justices of the Peace for Queensland.

Several people who had witnesses to the unfolding events from their camp sites on the creek bank were called and sworn in after taking the oath.

The first of them was John Smith who testified that he was camped on the Laidley side of Sandy Creek at about five o'clock on the Thursday afternoon in question.

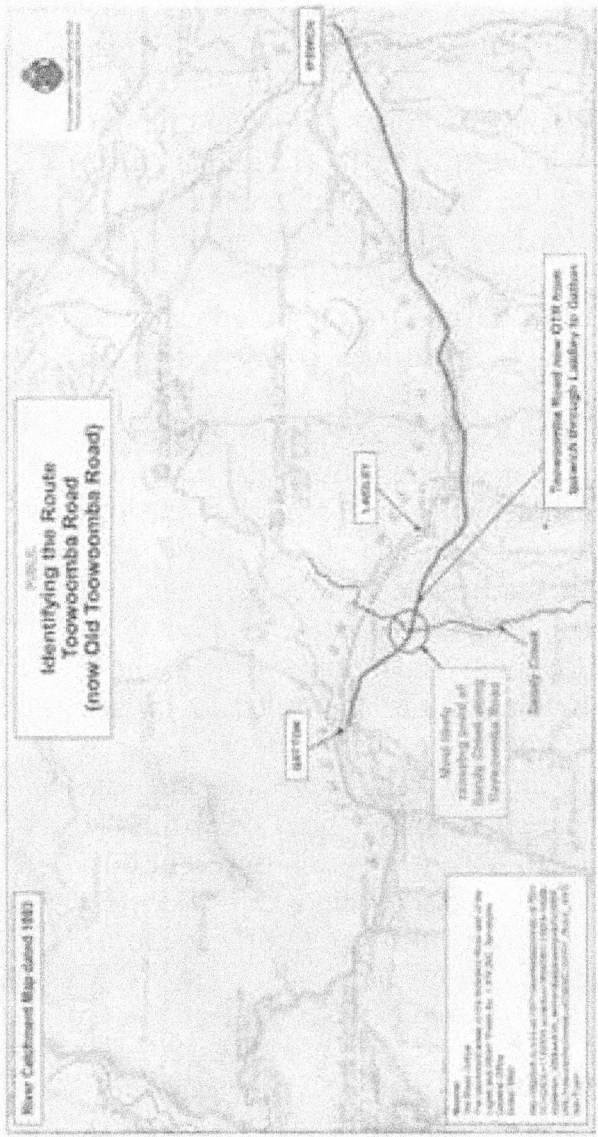

A map showing the location of the incident at Sandy Creek

'While I was there, I saw deceased Matthew Connelly, whose body I now recognise riding along the road from Laidley,' he said. 'When he came up to the camping place I spoke to him and told him the creek was too high. He said it was a little higher than usual, but he was determined to press on. He asked for a knife which he borrowed from a young man, also a traveller, to cut a cord which he had, using it to tie two parcels across his chest.

'He then took the creek. After getting in about a horse's length into the water, he and the horse were both swept off the logs forming the crossing place. Nearing the opposite bank the deceased, by pulling on the reins, brought the horse over on to its back. Connolly then floated down about three hundred yards. We called to a black fellow* who was tending a flock of sheep on the plain. He went in the water but did not succeed in getting hold of Connolly, but he did manage to bring out a tin box. The deceased disappeared and I saw no more of him until today in possession of the police.'

* *This Indigenous shepherd was never identified nor formally thanked for his bravery in trying to rescue the drowning policeman.*

Mr Smith was re-called and, in answering a question from Sergeant Curry, said, 'To the best of my knowledge and belief the deceased was perfectly sober. I saw no signs of liquor upon him.'

William Jenkins was then duly sworn. He stated, 'I identify the body of Matthew Connelly. I was in camp on Sandy Creek on Thursday the twenty-ninth. I saw the deceased take the creek. When he had got almost across, he pulled the head of the horse and caused the horse to turn over upon him. The deceased let the horse go and the stream carried him (the deceased) down. I followed him and saw a bough hanging in the water. I called out to him to look out for it. He made a catch at it but missed. I then called a black fellow shepherding sheep nearby who came up and, as soon as he got his clothes off, jumped in but missed the deceased who was carried down.

'The black fellow came out and went further down the bank to make a second trial, but the deceased disappeared. The black fellow did not go in again. The last time I saw the deceased he was about two hundred and fifty yards below the camping place. I followed down the creek and saw a small tin case floating on top of the water which the black fellow caught hold of.

'The deceased did not appear again. I returned to the camp and next morning, as soon as we could cross the creek, I went to Gatton and gave information to Sergeant Curry there.'

Jackson Curry, sergeant in charge of the Gatton Police, verified that the deceased Matthew Connelly was a constable attached to that station.

He said, 'On Sunday the twenty-fifth, Connolly left his quarters on escort duty with a prisoner to Ipswich. On Friday morning I received information that he was drowned at Laidley Creek on his return to Gatton. I immediately proceeded to Sandy Creek with Constable Latimer and made a strict search for the body in the creek. I instructed Latimer to keep to one side of the creek while I stayed on the other in order to examine it thoroughly.

'About a mile down I found the body entangled in a tree in the middle of the creek. I recovered the body and managed to get it onto the shore. As soon as I could I had it removed to Laidley where it now lies. Upon examining his person I found one five pound note, one sovereign, one half sovereign, ten shillings and sixpence in silver, two pence in coppers, which I now produce. There were two small vials of medicine, one of which was addressed to

Mrs Curry, my wife. I had asked him to get it for my wife from Doctor Rowlands.

'With the creeks being all up, I was unable to get to Mr W Rawson JP, the nearest magistrate to tell him in person what had happened, but I did manage to have the information passed to him.'

Sergeant Curry also said the deceased had been a teetotaler since the seventh of June. 'That was the last time; I have not known him to taste liquor since.'

Then, as the proceedings came to an end, Mr Rawson authorised the sergeant to cause the internment of the body of the late Matthew Connelly.

Queensland
DEATH CERTIFICATE

Matthew Connolly's death certificate

Chapter Six:
Outcomes

AT CONSIDERABLE personal expense, Catherine Connolly arranged for her husband's body to be taken from Laidley to Ipswich, intending to secure the services of the local priest to bury him.

Maintaining her own Catholic faith, she was shocked to learn more heartache was about to come her way. The stubborn and unforgiving priest added to her misery by not only refusing to attend the funeral, but also forbidding internment of the body in consecrated ground. To make matters even worse, the person she had hired to help her bring the body from Laidley did not arrive in Ipswich until dusk on the evening of the funeral.

Matthew's religious faith had lapsed somewhat during his time at Gatton. His widow's faith was dented when, instead of adhering to established Catholic funeral rituals, the priest abandoned her. There was no liturgy nor rite of committal which, at the conclusion of the funeral service, should have been the final act in caring for the body of the deceased.

Poor Catherine was afforded none of this, but was left to fend for herself. Apart from his widow, a couple of off-duty constables from Ipswich also turned up to farewell their brave, dedicated comrade. One of those who *did* attend described Matthew's funeral as being more melancholy than his actual death.

Matthew was eventually laid to rest in an unmarked grave in an Ipswich cemetery. To this day, despite extensive research, his final resting place cannot be located.

The local constables said their goodbyes and returned to their station. By then night had fallen and the weather was turning cold. Catherine was bewildered and confused.

The person who had conveyed her husband's body to Ipswich suggested they should get going. He offered to take her back to Gatton in the dray that had recently held the body of her dead husband. Although, before departing Gatton, she had given strict instructions to her two oldest children to look after the younger ones, be good and await her return, she was afraid something could go wrong.

Constable Connolly left behind a wife and six children. Now what?

Catherine was nearly destitute. Lieutenant-Colonel Gray had expressed concern for her wellbeing in his letterer to the Ipswich Magistrate following Matthew's death.

Gray had written: *The accident is doubly unfortunate as he leaves a wife and six, totally unprovided* (sic) *for children; they being too young to do anything for their own support. It would be an act of charity on the part of the Government if any relief could be extended to her as she and her family will be otherwise utterly destitute.*

Although, no formal charitable organisation was ever established, she managed to carry on; there were enough sympathetic community members and serving police officers to care for her.

She survived the hardships, and in 1863 married Patrick Feeney with whom she bore another three children. Catherine died in the Ipswich Hospital on 3 April 1907 and was buried in the Ipswich Cemetery.

Chapter Seven:
Tributes

MATTHEW'S OLD friend Lieutenant-Colonel Gray was one of those lamenting the policeman's passing. On 1 September 1861 he wrote to the Magistrate in Ipswich.

I have the honour to state that Ordinary Constable Matthew Connolly of B Division of the Metropolitan Police of this District was unfortunately drowned in returning to Gatton from when he had come to this place on duty.

Had I been aware that he proposed returning on Thursday, the day on which the melancholy accident happened, I would have prevented him, as I knew the creeks were swollen and his doing so would be attended with danger.

The poor man met his death in his anxiety to deliver medicine with which he was entrusted to the lady of one of the Magistrates of the District who was dangerously ill.

Gray

A note, hand-written at the bottom of the letter asked for a receipt and a request that the Police Magistrate be made aware, and that the matter will be brought to the attention of the Honorable Colonial Secretary. A further note said the Police

Magistrate in Ipswich was advised of the incident on 18 September 1861. Yet another postscript queried if it was deemed appropriate, and part of the constable's duties to go to Ipswich to fetch medicine for the sick wife of one of the magistrates.

The story of Constable Connolly could have ended right here if not for the efforts of his great, great granddaughter Juanita Keegan. In 2005 Mrs Keegan contacted the Queensland Police requesting a memorial of some kind be established to perpetuate Matter's contribution to the fledgling state of Queensland. Her correspondence was passed to a senior officer for consideration and approval.

Toowoomba-based Inspector Brett Schafferius (now Assistant Commissioner) took up the cause and began to lobby for Connolly's death to be officially recognised by either New South Wales or Queensland Police as having occurred while on duty.

'Connolly was serving as a police officer before the official establishment of both the New South Wales and the Queensland Police Forces, so he had not been recognised as dying on duty by the criteria of that time. He was not initially recognised as a fallen police officer because he served during the interim period of Queensland separating from

New South Wales and the creation of the then Queensland Police Force in 1864.

'However, Queensland was eventually established as a state, and as Connolly died while executing Police duties for the people of Queensland, he can be recognised as having died while performing the duty of a Queensland Police Officer.

'A plaque has been created to recognise his position as a member of B Division of the Metropolitan Police for the Ipswich District at the time of his death,' Assistant Commissioner Schafferius said.

The first police officer to be killed while on duty in Queensland was also the most recent to be recognised for making the ultimate sacrifice while serving his community.

Although Constable Matthew Connolly drowned on 29 August 1861 while risking his life trying to deliver medication for two seriously ill women, he was not initially recognised as a fallen police officer, all because he was serving during the interim period of separation from New South Wales. The then Queensland Police Force was not formed until 1864. The situation was later rectified when Constable Connolly's name became the one hundred and thirty-fifth to be included on the Queensland Police Service Honour and

Remembrance Rolls. This move was celebrated by family members, with about seventy descendants attending a memorial ceremony in August.

'They were absolutely overwhelmed to know that the Queensland Police Service have given his death the recognition he deserved, and are extremely appreciative of the actions taken to make this happen,' he said. 'It is rewarding to realise the actions of Constable Connolly, while in service of the people of Queensland, can be recognised even after his death so many years ago. It's a clear indication of the dedication the Service has towards recognising all police who have lost their lives in the line of duty, no matter when or where,' Mr Schafferius said. 'To my knowledge he was never honoured in any way for having given his life while serving his community.'

Tom Olsen, a retired police inspector, and Connolly's great, great grandson said it was an honour knowing that the constable could now be recognised as the first officer to have died in the line of duty in Queensland.

'It is wonderful that after all these years his service will not only be remembered across the state, but also in Canberra,' Mr Olsen said. 'Constable Connolly was originally appointed by a Police Magistrate as the watch house keeper at Gatton where part of his duties required him to escort prisoners to Ipswich. Even though I write of a distant relative, I conclude that history was not kind to Constable Matthew Connolly. However I will always remember him as a police hero of the past.

'He had finished an escort trip to Ipswich on 25 August 1861 when a doctor asked him to obtain medication from Ipswich for the gravely ill Lady Joshua Bell and the sick wife of his station sergeant.

'By the time Constable Connolly left Ipswich on the 29th of August, heavy rain had fallen in the region causing high water levels in the local creeks and streams. He arrived at the flooded Sandy Creek crossing near Laidley about five o'clock that day where a man who was camped at the crossing told Connolly the water was too high.

'Determined to continue, Connolly entered the creek on horseback. However, after a short distance he and his horse were swept off the crossing. The police officer lost control and grip of his mount; they became separated. The horse made for the opposite bank while Constable Connolly floated downstream for about three hundred metres. Bystanders desperately tried to rescue him but he disappeared from view.

The story of Constable Connolly would have ended right here if not for the efforts of his great, great granddaughter Juanita Keegan. In 2005 Mrs Keegan contacted the Queensland Police Museum requesting a memorial of some kind be established to perpetuate Matthew's contribution to the fledgling state of Queensland.

Mrs Keegan said, in her correspondence, the forgotten policeman only received the recognition he deserved after she started researching her family history.

'I was not told a great deal about him as a child,' she said. 'For a long time all I knew was that he was a policeman and he had drowned. It was only fairly recently that found out what really happened.

'After Matthew's body was recovered, his widow Catherine had it taken to Ipswich for burial but was refused Roman Catholic rites by the priest who also forbade his internment in consecrated ground.'

Mrs Keegan continued: 'Retired Magistrate Lieutenant-Colonel Gray attempted to obtain some financial relief for Catherine and her six children, but this was refused on the ground that perhaps it was not part of his duty to be delivering medicine for the wife of one of the magistrates, even though he was returning home after delivering a prisoner to Ipswich.

'Unfortunately, because his death occurred at the time of changeover of police forces between the two states, his death was never officially recognised by either police force until 2006. The Queensland Police Force was not officially gazetted until 1864.'

It took many years of research and hard work for Mrs Keegan before she eventually convince the powers that be to recognise Constable Connolly as a police officer who died while performing his duties. His name is now engraved at the top of police memorials at Ipswich, Brisbane and Toowoomba.

Mrs Keegan's persuasive correspondence was passed to a senior officer for approval.

With Queensland eventually becoming established as a state, and as Connolly had died while executing police duties for the people of Queensland, he could be regarded as having died while performing the duty of a Queensland Police Officer.

Further honours were bestowed when Constable Connolly's name became the one hundred and thirty-fifth to be included on the Queensland Police Service

(QPS) Honour and Remembrance Rolls. His name was also added to the Toowoomba Police Memorial.

Such action was celebrated by family members, with about seventy descendants attending the memorial ceremony. 'They were absolutely overwhelmed,' Assistant Commissioner Schafferius said. 'The Queensland Police Service has not given his death the recognition he deserved; his descendants are extremely appreciative of the actions taken to make this happen. It is rewarding to realise the actions of Constable Connolly, while in the service of the people of Queensland, can be recognised so long after his death. It's a clear indication of the dedication the Service has towards recognising all police who have lost their lives in the line of duty, no matter when or where.'

QPS Southern Region Police Chaplain Jeff Bails sought public help to establish the exact location of the drowning tragedy to enable a memorial service to be held on Police Remembrance Day. It has since been determined that the creek crossing at Glen Cairn as shown on the included map was where it happened.

In 2021 Chaplain Bails said the twenty-ninth of August that year marked a milestone in Queensland Police history. 'That was the hundred and sixtieth anniversary of the death of Constable Matthew Connolly, believed to be the first Queensland Police officer to die while performing his duty. He was the watch house keeper at Gatton who lost his life while returning from Ipswich on duty, and attempting to cross a flooded creek on horseback,' he said. 'Normally he would have waited for the floodwaters to recede, however he had been asked to deliver urgent medicine for two women on the other side of the creek. The next day when Connolly's body was recovered, the medicine was retrieved and delivered to the women.'

Constable Connolly's final resting place in the Ipswich General Cemetery has never been located. Despite that, he is memorialised on the Queensland Police Memorial in Brisbane, the National Police Memorial in Canberra, the Ipswich Police Station and adjacent to the Sangster Memorial in Brown Park, North Ipswich.

Because Connolly died during the period of changeover of police forces between New South Wales and Queensland, his death was not formally recognised until 2006. Separation of the two colonies occurred in 1859, and the Queensland Police Force was officially gazetted in 1864.

NOTE:

As the story slowly came to light, a number of newspapers took up the call.

Ken Blanch wrote an article for the Sunday Mail dated 11 July 1993: *Cop died a hero and no one cared.*

In the Queensland Police Union Journal of December 2005, Phil Hocken contributed a story entitled *The Cop Australia Forgot; the story behind Queensland's first police officer to die in the line of duty.*

Then, in September 2009, Queensland Times journalist Andrew Korner continued the narrative:

Until very recently, only a select few knew the story behind Queensland's first police officer to die in the line of duty.

'It's a clear indication of the dedication the Service has towards recognising all police who have lost their lives in the line of duty, no matter when or where.'

Chapter Eight:
Separation from New South Wales

THE SEPARATION of Queensland occurred in 1859 when the land that makes up the present-day State of Queensland was excised from the Colony of New South Wales to become the new, separate Colony of Queensland.

This is being touched on here to give readers an appreciation of the additional trauma created when neither colony (nor state) was prepared to acknowledge responsibility following Mathew's demise.

European settlement of Queensland began in 1824 when a convict outpost was established at Redcliffe. The settlement was transferred to the north bank of the Brisbane River the following year and continued to operate as a penal establishment until 1842, when the remaining convicts were withdrawn and the district opened to free settlement. By then squatters had already established themselves on the Darling Downs, far distant from the seat of the New South Wales Government in Sydney. Agitation soon began for the creation of a separate northern colony which could look after local interests.

Leading the call of those seeking representative government was the Reverend John Dunmore Lang, member for Moreton Bay in the New South Wales Legislative Council. Lang's motion for the creation of a northern colony in 1844 was defeated in the Council by twenty-six votes to seven. Matters were held in abeyance until 1850 when the British Parliament passed the Australian Colonies Government Act, which enabled the creation of new Australian colonies with a similar form of government to New South Wales. In other words, they would have a bicameral parliament watched over by a vice-regal representative. Importantly, specifically mentioned were Port Phillip and Moreton Bay as districts which were likely to become colonies in the foreseeable future.

The Act inspired Lang to renewed efforts; between 1851 and 1854 he held nine meetings to gain further support for separation. He was, however, preaching to the converted as the inhabitants of the northern district had been increasingly neglected by the government in Sydney.

Yet while they could reach consensus on the need for separation, whether a new colony would be free or unfree became a divisive issue. Lang and the majority of townspeople supporters favoured free immigration. The squatting fraternity, all powerful and heavily reliant on cheap labour, advocated a renewal of convict transportation. However, urban growth in Brisbane and Ipswich finally dictated for the former.

But there was still disagreement over where a new capital should be located. Brisbane, Toowoomba, Rockhampton, Cleveland, Gayndah, Gladstone and Ipswich were all potential candidates favoured by parochial interests. Brisbane eventually emerged victorious, and the reality of a new colony moved a step closer in 1856, when the British Government agreed the time was ripe for the creation of a new northern colony.

Among other things there was uncertainty over the location of a southern border. Lang was among many others who believed the Northern Rivers should become part of a northern colony; the New South Wales Government disagreed, and when Queen Victoria finally signed the Letters Patent to create Queensland on 6 June 1859 at Osborne House, the border was fixed at twenty-eight degrees south.

The following month, unofficial news was received that the Secretary of State for the Colonies, Sir Edward Bulwer-Lytton, had appointed Sir George Bowen to be the colony's first Governor of Queensland.

Bowen had recently served as Britain's Lord High Commissioner of the Ionian Islands near Greece, and had a distinguished career in the Colonial Office. His time in Greece was fruitful in more ways than one.

While both the Letters Patent and the Order-in-Council appointing Bowen as Governor were duly published by the New South Wales Government, separation could not be accomplished until the Letters Patent had also been published in Queensland. Letters patent are a legal instrument in the form of a published written order issued by a monarch, president or other head of state. Among other things they are used for the creation of government offices, to grant city status or coats of arms. They are also issued for the appointment of representatives of the Crown.

As Governor Bowen was due to arrive on 6 December 1859 with the actual Letters Patent formally proclaiming the new colony, a reception committee was organised as early as September to arrange the celebrations.

A special ensign, known as the Queensland Separation Flag, was unfurled and flown in Brisbane on 10 December 1859 to mark Queensland's separation from the southern state. The document authorising the Proclamation of Queensland was read by Governor George Bowen on the same day. Also, on that day he and Lady Bowen were greeted by an estimated crowd of four thousand exultant colonists when they stepped ashore at the Botanic Gardens in Brisbane. They were then conveyed by carriage to the temporary Government House, a building which now serves as the deanery of Saint John's Cathedral. After ascending to the balcony, the resident Supreme Court Judge, Justice Alfred Lutwyche administered Governor Bowen's oath. After that, the newly appointed Colonial Secretary read the Queen's Commission to the assembled throng. Formalities concluded with the proclamation of the Letters Patent.

On 10 December 1859, Bowen also appointed an Executive Council to operate as a provisional government until a parliament had been elected. Under the terms of in May 1860 for a term of five years. Bowen was to appoint their successors for life, and from the outset the nominee character of the Upper House proved highly unpopular. Attempts to amend the Constitution to make the Upper House elected were to continue until the Legislative separation, however, it was left for Sir William

Denison, Governor of New South Wales, to appoint eleven members to the first Queensland Legislative Council was finally abolished in 1922.

The Queensland Police Force (Service), as it exists today, came into being on New Year's Day 1864. It was established by the Queensland Government with a strength of 287 officers serving a population of 61,467. David Thompson Seymour was appointed as Acting Commissioner; later becoming Commissioner.

With the establishment of the Queensland Police Force, the government took steps to ensure its officers behaved and dressed in an appropriate manner. Rules for the general government and discipline of the members of the Police Force were published in the Queensland Government Gazette, 'in order that it may be conducted upon one uniform system and that its members may not be embarrassed in the execution of their several duties from want of proper instructions'.

The government of the day agreed to supply police with work clothing on the condition that the wearer was responsible for the uniform's care. Uniforms were inspected before the officers received their monthly salary, and money was deducted if they were not found to be in 'good and serviceable order'. Financial difficulties being experienced during those timed resulted in uniform supplies being delayed. Due to these delays, police officers often had to turn out in civilian clothes. Then, when the uniforms *did* arrive, they were generally ill-fitting and made from poor quality material.

The uniform worn by these police officers at that time was a dark blue jacket and top with a forage cap, supplied by the New South Wales Police. Transport in the 'settled' areas of the new colony was mainly on foot; in the unsettled areas it was on the back of a horse.

Conditions were rather harsh. Police often had to work a seven-day week, and were entitled to every second Sunday off. However, they rarely really benefit from such an arrangement. Officers worked a minimum nine-hour day and often more when required. There was no paid overtime; leave was infrequent. In the period between separation from New South Wales to 10 December 1859, and with the Queensland Police Force coming into existence on 1 January 1864, officers were grouped into local police areas under the direction of magistrates appointed by the Queensland Government. However, policing and law enforcement in

Queensland remained under New South Wales' legislation, policy and procedures. Magistrates had the authority to appoint additional members to the force as necessary.

At the time of separation, Morton Bay was a northern outpost of New South Wales, policed by officers from the parent colony. Separation saw many New South Wales police who were stationed in what was to become Queensland electing to stay on when things settled down. Connolly was one of those who decided to stay on and made up the police presence in Queensland during the transitionary days between 1859 and 1864.

NOTE: Brisbane's football venue, Lang Park is named in his honour.

*Uniform worn by all Queensland police officers
in the mid-1800s*

Letters Patent erecting Moreton Bay into a Colony under the name of Queensland and appointing Sir George Ferguson Bowen KCMG to be Captain General and Governor in Chief of the same

VICTORIA by the Grace of God of the United Kingdom of Great Britain and Ireland Queen Defender of the Faith To Our trusty and well beloved Sir George Ferguson Bowen Knight Commander of Our most distinguished Order of Saint Michael and Saint George Greeting Whereas by a reserved Bill of the Legislature of New South Wales passed in the seventeenth year of our Reign as amended by an Act passed in the Session of Parliament holden in the eighteenth and nineteenth years of Our Reign entitled "An Act to enable Her Majesty to assent to a Bill as amended of the Legislature of New South Wales to confer a Constitution on New South Wales and to grant a Civil List to Her Majesty" it was enacted that nothing therein contained should be deemed to prevent Us from altering the boundary of the colony of New South Wales on the north in such manner as to us might seem fit And it was further enacted by the said last recited Act that if we should at any time exercise the power given to us by the said reserved Bill of altering the northern boundary of our said Colony it should be lawful for us by any Letters Patent to be from time to time issued under the Great Seal of our United Kingdom of Great Britain and Ireland to erect into a separate colony or colonies any territories which might be separated from our said colony of New South Wales by such alterations as aforesaid of the northern boundary thereof and in and by such Letters Patent or by Order in Council to make provision for the Government of any such separate colony and for the establishment of a Legislature therein in manner as nearly resembling the form of Government and Legislature which should be at such time established in New South Wales as the circumstances of such separate colony would allow and that full power should be given by such Letters Patent or Order in Council to the Legislature of such separate Colony to make further provision in that behalf.

Now know you that we have in pursuance of the powers vested in us by the said Bill and of all other powers and authorities in us in that behalf vested separated from our colony of New South Wales and erected into a separate colony so much of the said colony of New South

Wales as lies northward of a line commencing on the sea coast at Point Danger in latitude about twenty eight degrees eight minutes south and following the range thence which divides the waters of the Tweed Richmond and Clarence Rivers from those of the Logan and Brisbane Rivers westerly to the great dividing range between the waters falling to the east coast and those of the River Murray following the great dividing range southerly to the range dividing the waters of Tenterfield Creek from those of the main head of the Dumaresq River following that range westerly to the Dumaresq River and following that river (which is locally known as the Severn) downward to its confluence with the Macintyre River thence following the Macintyre River which lower down becomes the Barwon downward to the twenty ninth parallel of south latitude and following that parallel westerly to the one hundred and forty first meridian of east longitude which is the eastern boundary of South Australia together with all and every the adjacent Islands their members and appurtenances in the Pacific Ocean. And do by these presents separate from our said colony of New South Wales and erect the said territory so described into a separate Colony to be called the colony of

Queensland. And whereas we have by an order made by us in our Privy Council bearing even date herewith made provision for the Government of our said colony of Queensland and we deem it expedient to make particular provision for the Government of our said colony. Now know you that we reposing especial trust and confidence in the prudence courage and loyalty of you the said Sir George Ferguson Bowen of our especial grace certain knowledge and mere motion have thought fit to constitute and appoint. And do by these presents constitute and appoint you the said Sir George Ferguson Bowen to be during our will and pleasure our Captain General and Governor in Chief in and over our said colony of Queensland and of all forts and garrisons erected and established or which shall be erected and established within our said colony or in its members and appurtenances.

And we do hereby authorise empower require and command you the said Sir George Ferguson Bowen in due manner to do and execute all things that shall belong to your said command and the trust we have reposed in you according to the several powers provisions and directions granted or appointed you by virtue of our present commission and of the said recited Bill as amended by the said recited Act and according to our Order in our Privy Council bearing even date herewith and to such instructions as are herewith given to you or which may from time to time hereafter be given to you under our Sign Manual and Signet or by our Order in our Privy Council or by us through one of our Principal Secretaries of State and according to such laws and ordinances as are now in force in our said colony of New South Wales and its dependencies and as shall hereafter be in force in our said colony of Queensland. And whereas it is ordered by our said Order made by us in our Privy Council bearing even date herewith that there shall be within our said colony of Queensland a Legislative Council and a Legislative Assembly to be severally constituted and composed in the manner in the said Order prescribed. And that We shall have power by and with the advice and consent of the said Council and Assembly to make laws for the peace welfare and good government of our said colony in all cases whatever And it is provided by the above recited Act that the provisions of the Act of the fourteenth year of Her Majesty chapter fifty nine and of the Act of the sixth year of Her Majesty chapter seventy six intituled "An Act for the Government of New South Wales and Van Diemen's Land which relate to the giving and withholding of Her Majesty's assent to Bills and the reservation of Bills for the signification of Her Majesty's pleasure thereon and the instructions to be conveyed to Governors for their guidance in relation to the matters aforesaid and the disallowance of Bills by Her Majesty shall apply to Bills to be passed by the Legislative Council and Assembly constituted under the said reserved Bill and Act and by any other Legislative Body or Bodies which may at any time hereafter be substituted for the present Council and Assembly" Now we do by virtue of the powers in us vested hereby require and command that you do take especial care that in making and passing such laws with the advice and consent of the said Legislative Council and Legislative Assembly the provisions regulations restrictions and directions contained in the said Acts of Parliament and in Our said Order made in Our Privy Council bearing even date herewith and in Our instructions under Our Sign Manual accompanying this Our Commission or in such future Orders as may be made by Us in Our Privy Council or in such further instructions under Our Sign Manual and Signet as shall at any time hereafter be issued to you in that behalf be strictly complied with And whereas it is expedient that an Executive Council should be appointed to advise and assist you the said Sir George Ferguson Bowen in the administration of the government of our said colony.

Now we do declare Our pleasure to be that there shall be an Executive Council for Our said colony and that the said Council shall consist of such persons as you shall by instruments to be passed under the Great Seal of our said colony in Our name and on our behalf from time to time nominate and appoint to be members of the said Executive Council all which persons shall hold their places in the said Council during Our pleasure But we do expressly enjoin and require that you do transmit to us through one of our Principal Secretaries of State exemplifications of all such instruments as shall be by you so issued for appointing the members of the said Council And we do hereby strictly require and enjoin you in proceeding to any such suspension to observe the directions in that behalf given to you by our present or any future instructions as aforesaid. And in the event of the death or absence of you the said Sir George Ferguson Bowen out of Our said colony of Queensland and its dependencies we do hereby provide and declare Our pleasure to be that all and every the powers and authorities herein granted to you shall be and the same are hereby vested in such person as may be appointed by us by warrant under our Sign Manual and Signet to be our Lieutenant Governor of our said colony or in such person or persons as may be appointed by us in like manner to administer the Government in such contingency or in the event of there being no person or persons within our said colony so commissioned and appointed by us as aforesaid then our pleasure is and we do hereby provide and declare that in any such contingency the powers and authorities herein granted to you shall be and the same are hereby granted to the Colonial Secretary of our said colony for the time being and such Lieutenant Governor or such person or persons as aforesaid or such Colonial Secretary as the case may be shall exercise all and every the powers and authorities herein granted until our further pleasure shall be signified therein.

And we do hereby require and command all our officers and Ministers Civil and Military and all other the inhabitants of our said colony of Queensland to be obedient aiding and assisting unto you the said Sir George Ferguson Bowen or in the event of your death or absence to such person or persons as may under the provisions of this our Commission assume and exercise the functions of Captain General and

Governor in Chief of our said colony. And we do declare that these presents shall take effect so soon as the same shall be received and published in the said colonies. In witness of the sixth day of June.

By Her Majesty's command.

About the Author

JIM NICHOLLS was born in Cootamundra in southern New South Wales. Following 21 years' service with the Royal Australian Air Force, Jim moved to Laidley with his family in 1975 where he took up an administrative position at the nearby Queensland Agricultural College; now a campus of The University of Queensland. He then turned his hand to writing, becoming a regular newspaper contributor, historian and author. For many years he was the Laidley-based country correspondent for the region's major newspaper *The Queensland Times*. He also reported for Laidley's own newspaper, *The Valley Weekender*.

Jim has travelled the world in search of adventure and train travel, producing stories from the Trans-Siberian Railway, USA, UK, South America, Africa, China, Tibet, India, Myanmar, Ukraine and South-East Asia. And, of course his home country of Australia.

In 2003 Jim was awarded the Laidley Shire Council's Australia Day Cultural Award in recognition of his literary and journalistic contributions which did much to raise the profile of Laidley and surrounding districts. His many travel stories have appeared in a variety of magazines and other publications.

His interest has now turned to history, especially that concerning his local community.

He and wife Shar have two adult children and are the proud grandparents of two sturdy boys.

Laidley 2025

Also by Jim Nicholls

A Country Corps (A history of the Salvation Army in the Lockyer Valley);

The Runaway Rattler (A novel tracing the adventures of a lone traveller circumnavigating the world by train);

*Murder in the Rain (The true, local crime story of a 1933 murder);

Tales of Travel and Trains;

An Aussie in Asia;

The Magic of Myanmar (A pictorial journey through a golden land);

Africa, the train, the covenant (A train journey from Namibia to Pretoria interspersed with snippets of Southern African history);

Ukraine (Notes from a fractured land);

Taking the world by train;

*Glenore Grove and the body in the billabong (A re-write of Murder in the Rain).